Unsinkable
The Molly Brown Story

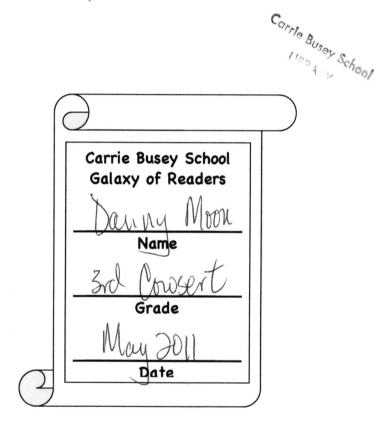

Unsinkable
The Molly Brown Story

A NOW YOU KNOW BIO

Joyce B. Lohse

Filter Press, LLC
Palmer Lake, Colorado

This book is for
our unsinkable
Jean Lohse

ISBN-13: 978-0-86541-081-7
ISBN-10: 0-86541-081-x
Library of Congress Control Number: 2006937225

Cover photo courtesy Colorado Historical Society, F4098.

Filter Press, LLC, P.O. Box 95, Palmer Lake, Colorado
www.filterpressbooks.com

Printed in Canada

Contents

*"It was Brown luck.
I'm the unsinkable Mrs. J. J. Brown."*

– *Rocky Mountain News,* October 28, 1932

Denver Post, October 28, 1932.

Introduction
April 15, 1912

In a moment a person's life can change forever. For Margaret Tobin Brown, known much later to the world as "Molly Brown," that life-changing moment arrived late in the evening of April 15, 1912. As she relaxed in her cabin aboard a luxurious cruise ship reading a book, a loud noise jolted her from her comfortable position. She immediately left her cabin to find out what was wrong.

Margaret Brown wrote her memories of that night a month later for the *Denver Post* newspaper. "I looked out and saw a man whose face was blanched, wearing the look of a hunted creature. In an undertone he gasped: 'Get your life-saver'."

Titanic, the unsinkable new luxury cruise ship on its maiden voyage, had hit an iceberg and was in danger of sinking.

"I immediately reached above and dragged [my lifesaver] out. Snatching up furs, I ran to A deck and there I found passengers putting on life belts. Strapping myself into one, I went up on the storm deck.

"On the storm deck we found a number of men trying to unravel the tackle of the [life]boats to let them down. We were told by an officer to descend to the deck below. We found the lifeboats there being lowered.

"Suddenly I saw a shadow and a few seconds later I was taken hold of and with the words, 'You are going, too,' I was dropped fully four feet into the lowering lifeboat.

"With but one man in the boat and possibly fourteen women, I saw that it was necessary for someone to bend to the oars. I placed mine in the rowlocks and asked a young woman near me to hold one while I placed the other one on the further side. She immediately began to row like a galley slave. All the time while rowing we were facing the starboard side of the sinking vessel.

"By that time E and C decks were completely submerged and the strains of music became fainter as though the instruments were filled up. Suddenly all ceased and the heroic musicians could play no more."

The foaming sea opened up as passengers lucky enough to get into a lifeboat watched from a distance as the great ship *Titanic* was pulled from below and disappeared from their sight.

Mrs. J. J. Brown found herself aboard Lifeboat Six. She knew that her life could easily end, but her will was strong, and she was not about to give in to the **formidable** challenges of that night. But the choice was not entirely up to her. In a lifeboat only half full of distraught women and a couple of men, bobbing on the frigid waters of the North Atlantic Ocean, the future of Margaret Brown and other passengers was quite uncertain. At that critical moment no one on the boat knew whether they would survive through the night or drown in those dark, icy, unforgiving waters.

Margaret Brown was a rich and confident woman who was accustomed to taking charge of a situation and seeing that things were done properly. Although she was as wet and cold as the others, she worked the oars and helped the other passengers with their comfort as they strained to row as far away from the sinking ship as possible.

To the survivors, an eternity seemed to pass before they spotted a light in the far distance across the icy water. The light was a signal from the *Carpathia,* a ship that had received a distress signal from the

Titanic. Although it was approaching to rescue the lifeboats, it was still miles away. The lights became easier to see as the ship approached, although the ocean waves became rougher and more difficult to navigate as the huge steamer approached the little lifeboats.

As dawn lit the sky, Margaret's lifeboat was the last one the *Carpathia* attempted to rescue. At first, the bobbing lifeboat was pulled away from the larger ship by the rocking waves. It took a great effort to steer the lifeboat close enough for the men in the steamer to reach. Only then were they able to remove its occupants and save them from danger. The *Carpathia* crew saved 866 people from the dark sea. But 1,492 people died that night, sinking with the grand cruise ship.

Once aboard the *Carpathia,* food, blankets, and medicine were offered to the survivors. Margaret did not seek the rest, relief, and comfort she craved. She could not rest. Margaret was surrounded by people who were frightened and anguished and far worse off than she. Many had lost loved ones. Others lost everything they owned when the ship sank.

Margaret used her extensive knowledge of foreign languages and cultures, along with her personal financial resources, to help other passengers. The lives of the survivors were no longer in danger, but for Margaret, her work had just begun.

1 Missouri Childhood

Located north of St. Louis, Missouri, on the banks of the Mississippi River, the bustling river town of Hannibal was Margaret Tobin's first home. She was born on July 18, 1867. Although many people now know her as Molly, her family called her Maggie, and she was known as Maggie or Margaret throughout her life.

Many **legends** were told about Margaret Tobin Brown's life. She thought the legends about her were "good stories," and she was known to make up a few tall tales of her own. One legend has it that shortly after she was born, a **cyclone** struck her hometown. According to the story, when the terrible storm hit, the frightened Tobin family ran to their storm cellar, leaving their tiny baby behind in the house. After the storm passed, baby Maggie was found safe in her crib, unafraid and thriving, surrounded by the wreckage of the house. The legend led some people to think this was a sign of strength and bravery to come later in Maggie's life.

The Tobins' home, which still stands, was a four-room cottage located on a dirt street in Hannibal's Irish shantytown. The street where the house stood was not paved until a century later, in the 1960s. Maggie grew up playing with her brothers and sisters, and attending school across the street. School was conducted in the home of her aunt, Mary O'Leary, her mother's sister. There were no public schools in

Photo courtesy of Vicki Dempsey

Molly Brown Birthplace & Museum in Hannibal, Missouri.

Missouri at that time, so Maggie, her **siblings,** and her cousins were taught by their aunt.

Hannibal was famous as a railroad crossroads and steamship harbor. It was the boyhood home of famous author Samuel Clemmens, who wrote under the **pen name** of Mark Twain. He introduced the town of Hannibal to the world through his classic books about the childhood pranks of Tom Sawyer and Huckleberry Finn. This active and attractive community was where many Irish Catholic immigrants made their home, worked hard, and raised their children. In spite of their poor circumstances, the river town gave them

Know More!

Myth Busters – Myths are stories that could be true but are not verifiable. Myths are usually considered to be true and go unquestioned. Several myths have become part of what people think they know about Margaret Tobin Brown. For example, one of the myths about Margaret Brown is that her name is not Margaret at all but Molly. The fact is she was never called "Molly" during her lifetime. You will discover other myths about "Molly" as you read. How much truth do you see in the myths? Were some of the stories simply exaggeration of actual events? Were other stories invented to make Margaret's life story even more exciting and interesting? Could the myths be partially true? Can you tell think of other examples of myths about other famous people? Hint: Did George Washington really chop down a cherry tree?

opportunities for adventure and strong family ties gave them strength and confidence.

In the 1870 U.S. census record for Hannibal, the Tobin household included the following members: John, 40, born in Ireland; Johanah (Johanna), 40, born in Ireland; Mary Ann, 14, born in Iowa; Katie (Catherine), 13, born in Vermont; and Daniel, 8, Maggy, 3, and William, 1, all born in Missouri. John and his wife, Johanna, had been a **widower** and **widow** when they met. They each brought a child from their first marriages to the family. Ellen (Helen) was born a year later, in 1871, making a family of eight.

Maggie's father, John, worked as a manual laborer for Hannibal Gas Works to support his family. After suffering through the **Irish Potato Famine** in Ireland, the family was happy to live in a town, and not have to depend on farming for survival. Maggie's mother, Johanna, kept up the house, took care of the children, and saw to their Catholic religious training. The recent end of the American Civil War, with its losses and after-effects, and the end of slavery, was still fresh in peoples' minds, memories, conversations, and households.

Maggie was a tomboy. As she grew up, she learned to catch fish and she liked to hike along the Mississippi

River with her brothers. The Tobin children liked to explore the bluffs and caves along the riverbanks. Margaret grew up to be an adventurous traveler and a lifelong student with a passion for reading and learning. As an adult, she made up for her lack of early schooling by reading extensively and taking classes in many subjects.

Although the family was happy, the Tobins were poor. Maggie admired wealthy, famous people. She yearned to be rich. She watched her father toil at his job and hoped she would someday be able to provide him with enough money so that he no longer had to work.

Once she reached thirteen years of age, Maggie was expected to get a job to help support the family. Her school years were over, as well as her childhood. She found a job in the Garth Tobacco Factory. The work was difficult and dirty, and the hours were long. There were no laws to prevent children from working six days a week, twelve hours a day. Although there was no longer time for play and adventure, there was plenty of time to dream of the day she could leave Hannibal and seek new places, sights, and adventures.

One version of her story tells that Maggie eventually became restless with her job and went to work as a housekeeper at the Park Hotel in Hannibal. For a vivacious, outgoing young woman, a fancy hotel was a more attractive place to work than the tobacco factory. Wealthy people who could afford the luxury of a hotel visit, or hotel living, which was fashionable at the time, fascinated her. She wanted to be like them.

Maggie maintained a lifelong admiration for Mark Twain and followed the career of Hannibal's famous author. It is possible Mark Twain met Maggie Tobin and talked to her, although she was fourteen years younger. Twain returned to his boyhood home in Hannibal several times, including on an 1882 visit. Could it have been Twain's colorful stories about Colorado and its mining districts that put the idea of going there herself in young Maggie's head? Some people think it was. Others think that a meeting between Maggie and the famous author was just another legend. Most likely, she admired Twain from a distance.

2 Leadville Days

aggie's sister Mary Ann was the first of the Tobin children to leave Hannibal for the lure of Colorado. Stories about riches and wealth to be found in Colorado's newly discovered mining districts reached Hannibal. Mary Ann and her husband, Jack Landrigan, answered the call of the mining life and moved to Leadville in 1883.

Boomtown life in Leadville was rough. The town overflowed with people scrambling to dig riches from the nearby hills. They stripped the trees from hills for lumber to use for buildings and to burn for heat. Busy, noisy dirt streets covered the town in mud or dust depending on the weather. Hazy, smoky air from the frantic industry made it difficult to breath. Hotels and boardinghouses were so overcrowded that guests had to take turns sleeping in eight-hour shifts.

The air was also thick with excitement. Some miners found riches, but most continued searching for their fortunes. Those who struck it rich kept the dream alive for those who did not. In some cases, fortunes were made and spent nearly overnight. It was wild and crazy and totally enchanting to lovers of adventure who were seeking their fortunes.

Maggie Tobin lived with her family in Hannibal until 1886, when she left home and traveled to Leadville to live with her sister. She was an attractive eighteen year old with red hair, a curvy figure, and a spirited, outgoing Irish personality. When her brother Daniel arrived at the wild mining camp, Maggie moved into his cabin and cooked his meals.

Before long, Maggie went to work in a **dry goods** store, sewing rugs and draperies. She worked at Daniels, Fisher and Smith's Emporium on Harrison Street, the busy main street in Leadville. The company later merged with the May Company across the street, and eventually became May D&F, then Foley's Department Store.

Another of the legends about Maggie says that Maggie worked as a dance hall girl in a saloon. It is unlikely that a young woman with Maggie's strong religious background would set foot in a Leadville saloon, let alone work in one. It is known that she disapproved of alcoholic beverages, so it seems unlikely that she would have considered working in a mining town saloon.

It did not take long for Maggie to catch the attention of a young man she met in a more acceptable place. As an Irish Catholic girl, Maggie quite naturally attended the Church of the Annunciation after she arrived in Leadville. James Joseph "J. J." Brown was a handsome young mining engineer, the son of an Irish immigrant, who attended the same church. Even though she was thirteen years younger, Maggie caught his eye at a church picnic, and he began to **court** her. During their years together, J. J. and Maggie enjoyed attending the theater. Their common interest might have begun at the Tabor Opera House in Leadville.

J. J.'s love for Maggie grew, and he began to think about marriage. There was only one problem—J. J. was not rich. As she laughingly said later, "I wanted a rich man, but I loved Jim Brown. I thought about how I wanted comfort for my father and how I had determined to stay single until a man presented himself who could give the tired old man the things I longed for him.

"Jim was as poor as we were, and had no better chance in life. I struggled hard with myself those days.

I loved Jim, but he was poor. Finally I decided that I'd be better off with a poor man whom I loved than with a wealthy one whose money had attracted me. So I married Jim Brown."

James J. Brown and Margaret Tobin were married in the Church of the Annunciation on September 1, 1886, after a six-month courtship. She was nineteen, and he was thirty-two. She said, "I gave up cooking for my brother, and moved to Jim's cabin, where the work was just as hard."

The next seven years in Leadville were the happiest of their lives. At first, the young couple lived simply in J. J.'s cabin in Stumpftown near his work. They moved to Leadville after Lawrence Palmer Brown, known as Larry, was born in 1887.

Their second child, Catherine Ellen, known as Helen, arrived in 1889. J. J. and Maggie settled into their busy household routine with two children. "And them were the happy days," as Maggie was fond of saying.

While J. J. worked as a mining engineer for the Ibex Mining Company, he developed a way to strengthen the walls of the mines with straw bales. This allowed the miners to dig deeper. In 1893, using this new method, he found a major strike in an overlooked mine, the Little Jonny. He was given one-eighth ownership in the

The Little Jonny Mine near Leadville, Colorado.

mine, which produced the largest ore strike yet in the mining district. The Browns were suddenly and fabulously wealthy. Margaret and J. J. had gone from rags to riches.

At the same time, Colorado and the country suffered a terrible economic slump when the United States government switched from silver to gold as the foundation to back the nation's currency. Silver was no longer needed nor purchased in large amounts to support the value of American money. Colorado silver mines closed and miners were suddenly out of work. Fortunes disappeared overnight. Through it all, J. J. Brown's Little

Jonny Mine continued to produce high-grade gold ore and the Browns became richer and richer.

The Little Johnny Mine produced enough gold to revive the mining industry in Leadville. To celebrate the mining camp's renewed prosperity, Leadville citizens decided to do something festive. In the winter of 1895 a grand ice palace was built. J. J. Brown pitched in $500 of his own money, and other wealthy citizens did the same. In the end, the Ice Palace cost $20,000 to build. The community hoped to attract large numbers of visitors and tourists, but an unseasonably warm December melted part of the ice palace. The palace stood in place through the winter, but failed to attract visitors.

Courtesy Colorado Historical Society J3569

Leadville's Ice Palace covered more than three acres and had spires sixty feet tall.

3 How the Other Half Lives

Money was no longer a problem. Margaret Brown, as she was now known as she matured, had a strong urge to live in the growing capital city of Denver, Colorado. Not to be denied, Margaret got her way when in 1894, she and J. J. purchased a fashionable mansion at 1340 Pennsylvania Avenue (now Pennsylvania Street) near Colorado's newly constructed capitol building. They paid $30,000, very expensive for the time, for the house and property.

Built five years earlier in 1889, the house was constructed of Colorado lava stone with red sandstone trim, and a modern, fashionable interior. It was one of the few homes in Denver to feature the latest conveniences such as electricity, central heat, and hot and cold running water. The Browns made their own improvements before moving in, such as the addition of a walkway to the front porch and a retaining wall in front. They decorated inside their new home with extravagant Victorian furnishings. Over the years, they collected decorative artifacts during their travels. When Margaret installed concrete statues of lions outside the house to protect it from danger, the house was known forever after as the "House of Lions."

Margaret was twenty-seven years old when she arrived in Denver and set her sights on making her place in Denver society, "to see how the other half lived." How could a small-town Irish girl go about impressing the socialites of this big city? Margaret had plenty of work to do, and she knew it. She needed fashionable clothing, and she needed to polish her manners and her poise. She hired tutors to help improve her grammar and writing skills. The mansion alone would not change her social status, although it allowed her to entertain at will. She planned lavish parties that spilled out onto the lawn while lively musicians played on the porch.

Margaret's intentions for involvement were not purely social. While she lived in Leadville, she was increasingly aware of the less fortunate. She saw how lack of concern for the safety of miners led to accidents

Photo by J. B. Lohse, 2003

The Browns' stately mansion, the House of Lions, was restored and opened as the Molly Brown House Museum in 1970.

MRS. JAMES J. BROWN.

In the Dress Worn by Her at the Slaves' Ball.

Mrs. James J. Brown wearing one of her elaborate imported ball gowns. The photograph was printed in the Denver Times, December 9, 1900.

that could cripple them, making them unable to work, or kill them and leave their families as destitute widows and orphans. She also actively supported **woman's suffrage**. **Progressive** Colorado was the second state, after Wyoming, to pass suffrage into law in 1893, giving women the right to vote.

For a few years after they arrived in Denver, Margaret and J. J. remained close and active together as a family. In the summer of 1896, the newspaper reported that the Browns traveled by ship, with their children, to Italy for the summer. Margaret's interest in the world was expanding.

Upon returning home to Denver, Margaret was inducted as a charter member of the Denver Woman's Club, an umbrella organization for many clubs, which provided outlets for Denver's socially concerned and responsible women. A few years later, she was elected head of the Art and Literature Committee of the same club. She also became associated with the Denver Woman's Press Club, and she and her husband joined the Denver Country Club.

Nine miles from their city mansion, the Browns built a summer home on Bear Creek near what is now Lakewood, Colorado. J. J. had purchased the land in parcels over time, beginning as early as 1895 while he was still in Leadville. The cornerstone on the house has the construction year 1897 chiseled on it, along with his name.

The country home was a retreat where the family could relax and enjoy fresh air and country life. Eventually, it evolved into a farm complete with livestock. The couple enjoyed horseback riding and used the latest methods for raising chickens and other live-

Photo by J. B. Lohse, 2006

The Brown family's summer house, which they called Avoca, is located at Yale and Wadsworth in Denver. The house is privately owned.

stock. The country house offered tranquility and rest from the cares and pollution of city life. The children could run and play and ride their ponies. The house was named *Avoca*, after one of Margaret's favorite poems, "The Meeting of the Waters," by Irish poet, Sir Thomas Moore.

The Meeting of the Waters

There is not in the wide world and valley so sweet
As the vale in whose bosom the bright waters meet
Oh! The last rays of feeling and life must depart,
Ere the bloom of that valley shall fade from my heart.
Yet was not that Nature had shed o'er the scene
Her purest of crystal and brightest of green;
'Twas not for soft magic of streamlet or hill,
Oh! no,—it was something more exquisite still.
'Twas that friends, the beloved of my bosom, were near,
Who made every dear scene of enchantment more dear,
And who felt how the best charms of nature improve,
When we see them reflected from looks that we love.
Sweet vale of Avoca! How calm could I rest!
In thy bosom of shade, with the friends I love best.
Where the storms that we feel in the cold world should cease,
And our hearts, like thy waters, be mingled in peace.

Society journalist Mrs. Leonel Ross O'Bryan, known to her readers as "Polly Pry," asked Margaret to send a letter to her explaining the meaning of *Avoca*. Polly Pry, who started out as the first female journalist for the *Denver Post,* published her own weekly newspaper. She included Margaret's letter without editing so readers would be amused by the spelling errors and lack of polish in her writing. Margaret did not see the humor in this, but was motivated to change the public's perception of her as an uneducated person. From then on, it was her goal to be portrayed as educated and culturally literate. Margaret forgave the letter joke, and a friendlier relationship developed with Polly Pry when they found they supported many of the same causes.

At one time, Margaret said, "I don't care what the newspapers say about me, as long as they say something." Ridicule of errors in her writing was not what she had in mind. While she worked on polishing her image, she continued to gain positive attention in the press for her charity work.

Margaret won over volunteers for her charities with invitations to her country home. Invited guests met at her city home at about 10 a.m. A horse drawn carriage took them to *Avoca*, where they wandered around the grounds. A delicious lunch was served. The newspaper described a table centerpiece consisting of a pyramid of fruit with a cluster of sweet peas at the top. On another occasion, bunches of red American Beauty roses were placed everywhere. After the business meeting and a pleasant day at *Avoca*, the carriage took the committee members back to Denver.

While fulfilling her dream to be rich, Margaret achieved another goal. When her parents took up residence in her home fulltime, she was finally able to provide her father with comfort during his golden years, after working so hard for so long. The family treasured her father as a favorite relative, as well as her mother, who helped with the household.

In the spring of 1899, Margaret's father died at her home. His body was returned to Missouri where he was buried near other family members. Her mother continued to live in the Brown home for some time.

After her father's passing, Margaret threw her energy into organizing a benefit bazaar for St. Joseph's Hospital. She achieved notable success as president of the charity. When donated prizes from the fair were left unsold for the charity, she organized a huge **euchre** card tournament to use up the prizes and to finalize the fundraiser. The card party was a novelty, and Denver society was intrigued. It was a huge success, and Margaret proved her ability to organize, manage, and carry out the large event. J. J. was there to help, acting as a judge at the card tournament.

The previous year, J. J. had suffered a small stroke. On his doctor's recommendation, he decided to retire from work, at least temporarily, and move to Ireland for four or five years. At the time, he told the *Rocky Mountain News,* "When I was in Ireland two years ago, I saw a little spot in the neighborhood of Killarney where I thought I could enjoy living. There is where I am going. No, I shall not build a castle, because I don't consider it a permanent move. There is a nice little private country hotel, and my wife and I shall live there. My wife owns our residence here, and that will be left in charge of friends. It will not be given up."

Margaret went with J. J. to Ireland, but neither stayed long. They returned to Colorado — J. J. to his mining business and travels, and Margaret to her social activities and interests. Their children attended the finest schools Denver had to offer, and the Brown household was again a vibrant, busy one. J. J. was forty-five years old and Maggie was thirty-two.

At the turn of the century, Colorado's population had grown to over half a million people. Before the next decade was over, cars would take over Denver streets where horses and buggies had dominated previously. Women were finding more productive community outlets for their energies.

Margaret Tobin Brown was more involved than ever Denver's social scene, and in organizing grand dances and balls for charity and the arts. Her efforts were generous, and

James J. Brown in an undated photograph published in the Denver Times, January 24, 1910.

she enjoyed the attention gained with her lavish gowns designed in the latest Paris fashions accented by her eye-popping jewelry.

Margaret and J. J., with their ongoing interest in opera and theater, were often seen and mentioned in the newspaper when they appeared in their "Brown Box" at the Tabor Opera House in Denver. Their children often attended plays and operas with them. The *Denver Times* said, "Mrs. Brown's vivacity and merry disposition is a most refreshing trait in a society woman of her position, for the smart set, any disposition to be natural and animated is quite frowned upon. Mrs. Brown's gowns are as original as her ideas and that's interesting, too."

In 1900, Mrs. J. J. Brown hosted a Christmas party at the Brown Palace Hotel for underprivileged children. The *Denver Times* newspaper printed a letter from her that year, describing her feelings about Christmas:

ANOTHER WHO IS JOYFUL BECAUSE THE POOR WILL BE FED AND CLOTHED THIS SEASON
by Mrs. J. J. Brown

This Christmas is going to be one of the very "happiest" of all my many Christmas days, and I'll tell you why. When I sit down to my Christmas dinner on Tuesday, I can enjoy it without the twinge of conscience that while I am eating there might be hundreds of unfortunate people who might be lacking even the necessities of existence. This year Denver is going deep in its pockets to provide a merry Christmas for everyone in the city, and it is very comforting to think that everybody may, if they wish, enjoy themselves. The Christmas festival provided by The Times will give hundreds of little tots just as much happiness as they can hold. Then Guggenheim's dinner at the Brown Palace for thousands of little children, and the various church trees and entertainments will gather together all the children of the city and what pleasure it is to see the dear little children so boisterously happy!

All of my Christmas days were happy ones, though, and I can recall a score or more, each of them distinguished by some particularly happy event. This Christmas, perhaps, is the happiest, because it is the one most fresh in my memory, and we always think the joy of the moment greater than that of the past.

4 Adventures Abroad

With travel becoming easier, Margaret was able to take college classes at schools in the East. In 1901, after enrolling her children in boarding schools in Europe and the East Coast, she attended the Carnegie Institute in New York. She took college-level courses to polish her education and literacy, and she learned to speak French fluently. As a result of her intense interest, she later helped organize the Alliance Francaise in Denver, dedicated to the study of French culture in the United States.

Margaret and J. J. broadened their travel experience further when they went around the world together, this time to the Far East, with visits to India and Japan. Margaret delighted in visiting and learning about different cultures. Exercising her flare for drama, she wore costumes, such as Japanese **kimonos,** to social events at home, treated friends to her new **yodeling** and folk dance skills after a trip to Switzerland, and played the **ukulele** for guests after visiting Honolulu, Hawaii.

In 1903, Margaret's sister-in-law, Daniel's wife, passed away, leaving four children behind. The Browns opened their hearts and home to them, taking in three nieces to raise as their own. Maggie was particularly close to her niece named Helen. Their nephew lived elsewhere, but visited often.

A project that benefited from Maggie's drive and energy was a grand Carnival of Nations. Inspired by the Browns' two visits to the St. Louis World's Fair in 1904, the carnival benefited the Cathedral of the Immaculate Conception, which was to be built at the corner of Colfax and Logan in Denver. Unfortunately, the church invested money in a Cripple Creek mining concern that did not pay off, depleting the church building fund and delaying construction. J. J. Brown and other business associates generously purchased land for the cathedral. Nellie Campion, wife of J. J.'s mining partner, John Campion, assisted Margaret with plans for the carnival. The Campions also donated large bells for the chapel towers.

The carnival featured outdoor displays presenting many countries in living-history style. Margaret's progressive ideas of honoring African, Chinese, and Native Americans with booths at the carnival caused a stir and were the subject of much conversation, but did nothing to hinder the carnival's success. The *Republican* newspaper made this comment: "Of all the members of the various committees, Mrs. J. J. Brown is the busiest. She is so busy that it is almost impossible ever to find her anywhere, and whatever success the fair attains will be due in no small degree to her energy."

While counting the money raised at the carnival, Margaret exclaimed, "If only I were a man!" She had earned respect for her community work. If she was not restricted as a woman to applying her skills to charity fund-raising, who knows what success she might have attained with other business endeavors.

In 1905, Margaret's mother died. She had been caring for her mother for some time in her home. Margaret again made the sad trip back to Hannibal, where her mother was buried next to her father.

A well-known legend described Margaret Brown as longing, without success, to enter the tight social circle of Mrs. Crawford Hill. Mrs. Hill's group was called the "Sacred Thirty-Six," named for the number of guests required to fill her bridge tables. Although Margaret might have wished to break into Mrs. Hill's tight circle of socialites, it was not for lack of friends and social involvement of her own. She achieved her place in society, just as she had hoped when she came to Denver, and she continued to improve her community as an **activist** and **philanthropist** on her own.

Margaret took unusual steps to help her friend, Judge Ben Lindsay, raise money to benefit the Juvenile Improvement Project. Their goal was to establish a juvenile court, and to provide a safe place for poor and homeless youngsters who had been in trouble with the law. To raise money, Margaret went to Cripple Creek. Using her mining experience from her Leadville days, she personally located an idle mine that could produce enough ore to raise money to help the children and she invested her money in it. When the mine yielded a profit, all the money went to her favorite charities.

Still Margaret was restless. She traveled to the West Coast for another charity event, then to Newport, Rhode Island, where she rented a home. She enjoyed her friendships there and acceptance among the wealthiest people in the country, and she began spending more time in Newport. In the meantime, J. J. spent his time in Arizona and California, hoping the warm, dry climates would improve his health.

Know More!

Names and Nicknames – People often use more than one name in their lifetime. Sometimes names are attached to them by other people. What names were used for and by Margaret Tobin Brown? Why? Do different names cause confusion? Are they important? What affect does newspaper reporting have on people's names and how they are perceived by the public?

Margaret was forty-three when she went east to Newport, surrounded by her friends. She again enrolled her children in East Coast boarding schools. Her time at the Carnegie Institute years earlier had left her hungry to learn and to travel. Her world was expanding beyond Denver, and beyond her husband.

On January 24, 1910, the large headline in the *Denver Times* read, "Report of Brown Divorce Is Denied by Mrs. Brown." The past few years had taken a toll on Margaret and J. J.'s marriage. He claimed they had been divorced, and she claimed they had not. Accusations flew between them. He claimed she was prone to excessive spending. She defended her extravagant lifestyle by saying that he encouraged her expensive purchases.

What happened to tear the Browns apart? Several explanations come to mind. They certainly had their

Margaret Brown at her fashionable best, about 1910 in Denver.

differences—Margaret's social flurry and social climbing did not appeal to J. J. He was in a flurry of another sort, staying away from home for long periods of time for business, in the company of his own friends and, possibly, other women.

Friends claimed that J. J.'s stroke made him prone to delusions and to blurting out rash statements. Margaret acknowledged they had separated and adjusted their living situation so his peculiarities would not disrupt the family. She also stated openly that their Catholic religion would never allow divorce as an option.

With their marriage in shambles, Margaret Brown suffered a nervous collapse. As she told the *Denver Times:*

> What I want to do most of all is to get away from Denver for awhile and all its painful associations. There has been no pleasure in being obliged to listen to all these reports and to have to be questioned about conditions of which I myself am only too sensitively conscious. And I do not care to talk about Mr. Brown and his condition, because it would be evidence of poor taste on my part.

I will only say this: that his peculiarities have made it necessary for me to reach an adjustment of finances, that we may live apart. I haven't the slightest doubt but what Mr. Brown has made statements to outsiders which intimated a divorce proceeding; and I haven't a doubt but that he actually declared there was a divorce. For in his condition, which this high altitude aggravates, he is liable to say anything.

To me, he has never uttered one word of divorce. He has not intimated even a separation. But he has absented himself from the house for months at a time and when he has come back, we have humored him by not asking any questions as to where he has been and what he has done. And he himself has never said anything. He has returned from an absence of months, just as though he had been gone during the day and was coming home to dinner and an evening with his family.

The children were almost grown, as were their cousins in the household—Grace, Florence, and Helen Tobin. Margaret's daughter, Helen, was twenty and her son, Larry, was twenty-two. In 1909, Larry met a young lady named Eileen while he was vacationing with his mother and sister in Grand Lake, Colorado. They were married in January 1911. His parents were not pleased, because he had not finished college and had no job or career. He took up mining in Cripple Creek, and by the end of the year, he and Eileen had a baby boy. Margaret Brown was a new grandmother.

In 1912, Margaret was vacationing and enjoying the sights of the world. Her daughter, Helen, who was enrolled in school at La Sorbonne in Paris, joined her during her a portion of her travels. Margaret also joined up with wealthy East Coast businessman John Jacob Astor IV and his wife, Madeleine, who was pregnant, in Cairo, Egypt. Margaret's adventures there included a ride on a camel and a visit with a fortuneteller, who warned her of danger and icy waters in her future.

In April, Margaret received word that her grandson was gravely ill. Concerned about her family, she decided to leave immediately for Colorado. She and Helen bought tickets to travel to New York, as did the Astors, aboard the giant luxury ship *Titanic* on its maiden voyage across the Atlantic Ocean. At the last minute, Helen stayed behind in France. Few people back home knew that Margaret boarded the giant ship without her daughter Helen. *Titanic* prepared to leave Cherbourg, France, transporting tourists, immigrants, and businessmen across the Atlantic Ocean to New York City.

5 Declared "Unsinkable"

When the *Titanic* luxury steamer hit an iceberg in the icy North Sea, nobody thought it would sink. It had been built with strength and safety features meant to make such a tragedy impossible. However, the ship, a "floating palace," would not survive the night. Many of the passengers and crew, unable to find space on the few available lifeboats, drowned in the frigid waters.

Disaster sometimes brings out unusual strength and courage in people. Margaret Brown busied herself by helping others into the lifeboats. She recalled, "The last boat was being lowered without me, but I was unafraid, as I felt that I could swim, but I would probably now be at the bottom of the fathomless sea were it not for two powerful men who picked me up like a child and dropped me into the lowering boat." Her fate was sealed. According to custom, women and children were placed first in the lifeboats, leaving behind many heroic men, standing calmly on deck or pacing back and forth as they smoked their cigars, while the ship slipped slowly into the sea.

Back in Denver, confusion reigned while newspapers sorted out lists of survivors and casualties while they received sketchy details of the tragedy by **wireless radio** far across the ocean. At first, it was thought that Mrs. Brown and her daughter, Helen, had both been onboard the ship. Then, to the relief of family and friends, it was learned that Mrs. Brown had somehow survived and that Helen had changed her plans and stayed behind, safe in Paris.

Mrs. Brown's account of survival in Lifeboat Six was printed in the *Denver Times*:

> There were but sixteen people in our boat and one of them, the quartermaster, was the most craven of cowards.
>
> All night long he sat shivering like an aspen in the prow of the boat and muttered in a monotonous, sing-song voice that we were lost, lost, lost, and at the cruel mercy of the waves. Once I threatened to throw him overboard, and for a moment

he was silenced. For hours, we rowed through the bitter cold and darkness, ever toward that phantom light far out on the great deep. The sky was studded with stars, the sea was calm and still with a fatal and indescribable beauty.

The Titanic, true pride of the ocean, after the shock staggered for a moment under her death blow and then; as we looked, the waves seemed to rise with caressing touch and draw her quietly down to her final resting place. The band played to the last. Brave men went to their death almost without a murmur. Then one long scream of agony arose and all was over…

The courage, calmness and endurance of those women during the long night hours of suspense and terror was almost supernatural.

Newspaper stories retold "Lady Margaret's" heroism in the lifeboat. She rowed heartily and encouraged the other women to sing and row, to keep their spirits up and to keep them from freezing. They pulled a man aboard from another lifeboat to help with the rowing. He was an engine stoker who was covered with soot and half-frozen. Margaret wrapped him in her furs to keep him from freezing to death and encouraged him to start rowing to help his circulation.

In a subdued and humble tone, Margaret told the newspapers, "Please don't say that I am a heroine. I did only the natural thing and not the heroic. I was the most fortunate woman on the boat. Although I lost all my worldly possessions, I lost no dear ones and I was healthy, strong, and self-possessed, so why shouldn't I have helped those poor, suffering foreigners and victims of man's greed?"

Her comments about greed were directed at White Star Line Managing Director J. Bruce Ismay. Margaret accused Ismay of having an obsessive desire to break the speed record for crossing the Atlantic. He pushed the ship faster and faster—much too fast through the dangerous iceberg fields of the North Sea. Margaret said, "He was speed mad, and paced the deck like a caged lion as the ship surged through the icy waters. His hand, deadly and terrible, was, figuratively speaking, on the throttle, and in his powerful selfishness, he cared not for human life."

When the ship sank, Margaret lost many personal items including gowns and jewels. Also lost were four cases of priceless artwork she had collected for the

Denver Art Museum. More importantly, she lost friends, including John Jacob Astor IV. The deadly sea did not discriminate between rich and poor. Rich society vacationers, such as Astor's wife, and poor European immigrants traveling to a new country lost precious family members. As she said, "It isn't who you are, nor what you have, but what you are that counts. That was proved in the *Titanic*."

When asked how she was able to survive the ordeal, Margaret said, "It was Brown luck. I'm the unsinkable Mrs. J. J. Brown." As unsinkable as she was, Margaret was deeply affected by the events of that night. As she looked around, she saw women and children, far from their homes, lost and terrified. The men in their families had died for a **principle.** As she described it, she did not agree with it one bit.

"Women first, is a principle as deep-rooted in man's being as the sea—it is world-old and irrevocable. But to me it is all wrong. Women demand equal rights on land—why not on sea? In times of safety, they cry out for equality with men—in terrible danger they turn to men for protection. It is only fitting that the women of America should erect a mighty memorial to the noble manhood among rich and poor that was sacrificed that we, the women might be here now."

The *Carpathia,* a ship traveling about fifty miles away from the *Titanic* tragedy, was the first to receive and acknowledge the distress message sent over the wireless radio and to come to the aid of the survivors. When the *Carpathia* arrived at sunrise and pulled the survivors aboard, Lady Margaret went to work. Because she knew several foreign languages, she could help the foreigners among the survivors. She shared clothing and money that she grabbed at the last minute before leaving her room aboard the *Titanic.* With so many people in need, there was no time to rest.

When the *Carpathia* arrived in New York, desperate families and friends scrambled to find their loved ones. Margaret was reunited at the docked rescue ship

The caption of this illustration in the Denver Post, *April 17, 1912, reads, "If the Empire State Express had struck the same object, the force of the impact would be 367,500 tons. It would take 37 of these to equal the force of impact of the Titanic."*

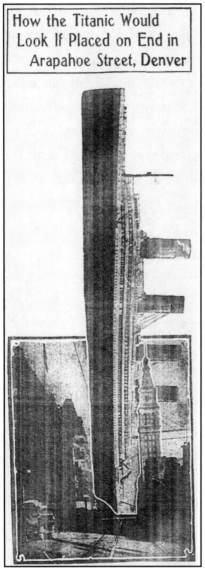

How the Titanic Would Look If Placed on End in Arapahoe Street, Denver

An illustration from the Denver Post, *April 16, 1912, attempts to illustrate the size of the* Titanic.

with her relieved brother, Daniel, and a New York friend, Mrs. Genevieve Spinner. In spite of her brother's and friend's worried protests, Margaret would not yet leave the ship.

She said, "God knows I can do little enough to save these poor souls around me that are out of their senses."

When newspaper reporters pushed to get photographs and stories, all Margaret would say was, "Tell my Denver friends I am safe." After her statement, she turned from the press and returned to the *Carpathia* to help.

Onboard the rescue ship, Margaret helped survivors write messages to relatives and used her own money to pay to send their messages by wireless radio. She organized a Survivors' Committee and had raised almost $10,000 by the time she left the ship. The money was used to pay the medical expenses of the injured and burial expenses for those who did not survive the rescue. Many passengers needed lodging until they could arrange to return home or join family.

Margaret was affected by the *Titanic* disaster in another way. She had a firsthand story to tell, and everybody wanted to hear it. That is, almost

Know More!

Wireless Radio – Guglielmo Marconi's wireless telegraph was a recent invention when the *Titanic* hit the iceberg. Marconi received the Nobel Prize for Physics in 1909 for his invention of the wireless signal telegraph. The wireless operator aboard the *Titanic* was able to send a distress message that the vessel was sinking and help arrived quickly. The new technology was also used to send the news of survivors to panicked relatives and the media. Without the wireless telegraph how would the news of the *Titanic* have reached the world? Trace developments in mass communications from 1912 to today's cell phones. If the *Titanic* sunk today, how would you learn of it?

Daily News, April 20, 1912

Newspapers ran front-page stories of Mrs. Brown depicting her as the hero of the Titanic disaster.

everybody. To her dismay, she was not asked to testify or share her version of the story before a Senate committee investigating the tragedy. Only two women were allowed to speak. But that did not keep Margaret quiet. She used her journalistic skills to tell her story. At first, the newspapers delighted in repeating Margaret's every detail of the disaster and the warm reception she had received at the Sacred Thirty-Six luncheon. Fame is fickle, and a few short months later, newspaper reporters accused her of being "an unsuccessful social climber." They were tired of her accounts of reading classic literature and her boring *Titanic* story. It did not matter. Mrs. J. J. Brown was unsinkable.

6 Unsettled but Inspired

On May 29, 1912, Margaret represented the Titanic Survivors' Committee when she presented a trophy to Captain Rostron and medals to the crew of the *Carpathia,* in honor of their heroic rescue of the *Titanic* survivors. Later, she helped erect a memorial in Washington, D.C., to honor those brave souls who lost their lives aboard the steamer.

Margaret regularly visited the graveyard in Nova Scotia where those who perished in the disaster were buried. The magnitude of the event never left her. Neither did her awareness of those less fortunate than herself. She spent the rest of her life in helping people in need and working for the rights for women and children. She seemed determined to use her second chance at life to make the world a better place.

Margaret Brown presented a trophy to Captain A. H. Rostron of the rescue ship, Carpathia, *and medals to his crew, on behalf of the Titanic Survivors' Committee.*

Margaret became more involved in politics. In Newport she worked for the national woman's suffrage movement. Encouraged by her friends in Newport, Margaret decided to run for the United States Senate. She had the support of Colorado suffragists. Many others did not support her bid for **Congress**. Her critics considered her efforts to be a rich woman trying to buy her way into public office. Men, as a group, were reluctant to support her because she was a woman. Easterners distrusted her uncultured western background, and Westerners distrusted her high-society eastern connections.

During the time she was considering running for Congress, a war that would develop into World War I was beginning in Europe. Margaret's response was to organize a regiment of female soldiers. Her position was clear. If women wanted equal rights, then they should carry weapons and fight with the men during times of war. Men resisted the idea, as did some women, and the press stirred the pot by asking how the women would march to war wearing long skirts. Her idea caused quite a stir, but Margaret figured her efforts to form a regiment would not be lost. If the women

Margaret Brown in a striking pose with furs and a walking stick in 1927.

were not allowed to serve in combat, they would be ready to serve in the Red Cross.

One of Colorado's darkest moments occurred in 1914, pulling Margaret's attention and efforts away from foreign wars to home. Immigrant coal miners in the Southern Colorado coalfields of Ludlow, northwest of Trinidad, went on **strike.** They would not return to work until they received higher wages and safe working conditions in the mines. When the miners and their families were removed from mining company housing to live in temporary tent cities, tensions ran high. The **militia** was brought in to maintain law and order.

On April 20, 1914, shots were fired and fire spread through the tent city. Seventeen people died that day—four men, two women, and eleven children. With the tent city burned to the ground, surviving families were left with nothing. Throughout the state there were cries of "Remember Ludlow"!

Margaret cancelled her travel plans and stayed in Colorado to aid victims of the tragedy that became known as the Ludlow Massacre. "I am here to relieve the suffering on both sides in this industrial war," she told the newspaper. "I do not wish to be allied on either side, capital or labor; but I want to help both.

Women on both sides are suffering. Women of the whole state must unite in giving aid to all."

Remembering the poverty and needs of mining families during her days in Leadville, Margaret sent first aid supplies and two hundred pairs of shoes to Ludlow. She was an inspiring public speaker and used that skill to draw attention to the plight and hardships of mining camp survivors. Working conditions and pay for miners eventually improved, but at the terrible cost of the Ludlow Massacre.

Meanwhile, Margaret's Senate campaign was losing momentum. Her supporters were divided by various issues and factions, and it was unlikely they could guarantee a party nomination. Troubles in Europe were leading up to World War I. Margaret was especially concerned about her sister, Helen, who was living in Germany with her husband who was a government official. In such a quickly changing world, Margaret's aspirations to national political office no longer seemed like a good idea. Instead, she chose to continue her work as an effective activist, drawing attention to important issues.

When the United States entered World War I in 1917, Margaret turned over her home in Newport to the American Red Cross to be used as a war hospital.

Her son, Lawrence, joined the army, and Margaret went to France to establish a relief station there. During the war, she traveled throughout France, helping war victims.

After the war, Lawrence was reunited with his family in Colorado. Margaret's daughter, Helen, was married to George Benziger in 1913. They had two boys, born in 1914 and 1917, and lived in New York. Margaret returned to New York where she turned her attention to helping soldiers who had been blinded in the war.

J. J. had been ill for years and lived in the warm Southwest. On September 5, 1922, J. J. Brown died, at the age of sixty-eight. Although they had lived apart for years, Margaret and J. J. never divorced. When he died, he left the family's finances in a jumble of confusion.

The next several years were spent in disagreement about the division of J. J.'s estate between Margaret and the rest of the family. It was a tense and uncomfortable time. Lawrence and Helen suddenly raised concerns about the extravagance of their mother's spending and about the amounts she donated to charities. The family went to court in Denver, and the matter should have been resolved. Legend has it that it was never resolved, but it was settled to a point that everyone could carry on with their lives.

During this period, Margaret Brown helped establish the first all-female "feminist coalition" for mine operations in Leadville. She had always taken a hands-on interest in mining in Leadville. By inheriting J. J.'s portion of the Ibex Mining Company, she was now owner of the Little Jonny Mine. Margaret joined forces with the widowed wives of J. J.'s partners, who were also shareholders in the mine, and encouraged them to take a more active interest in management of their mining shares. The board of directors took a dim view of the idea and continued management without giving up any control to the female mine owners.

7 Golden Years

Margaret rented out the House of Lions in Denver for many years while she continued to pursue her interests and her travels. She managed the care of the house long–distance by sending letters and telegrams with instructions to her housekeeper. Her bold, decisive handwriting and abrupt instructions were direct, yet kind. In one letter, she suggested that leftover money be used to plan a cookout for the household helpers.

Margaret faced danger and became a heroine once again in 1925. While she was staying at the luxurious Breakers Hotel in Palm Beach, Florida, a fire broke out. Fifty-eight-year-old Margaret took charge and led the guests to safety. The wealthy guests gathered outdoors wearing scant bedclothes. Their other clothing and possessions were lost in the fire. Fortunately, no lives were lost. Margaret lost belongings worth about $10,000.

Nevertheless, Margaret continued her adventures. A story in the *Rocky Mountain News* told of a potential romance in her life. The story announced her engagement to Duke Charto of France, who was seventy-six years old at the time. Within two days, Margaret had retracted the announcement saying, "Me marry that old geezer—never. Give me every time the rugged men of the West."

Although she traveled the world, Margaret was always drawn back to the places of her childhood and to Colorado. In Hannibal, Missouri, she established a memorial to author Mark Twain, who had died in 1910. In Denver, Margaret bought and restored the home of poet Eugene Field, scrubbing and painting the house herself. She donated it to the city to be used as a library and serve as a memorial to the poet. The Field House operated as a branch of the Denver Public Library until 1970.

Margaret studied acting for several months under the instructor of the famous actress Sarah Bernhardt. In 1929, the *Denver Post* reported that for her theatrical performance in *L'Aiglon,* she was awarded the Palm of the Academy of France, a cherished decoration given to few Americans.

In April 1932, Margaret Brown was awarded the French Legion of Honor. She received the award for her work with blind soldiers after World War I and for being an "overall good citizen." She received additional recognition from France for her long-term association with the country and for her appreciation of the French culture.

Age was catching up with Margaret. It was time for her to come home. She moved into the Barbizon Plaza Hotel, a chic and fashionable woman's hotel in New York City. There she had all the attractions of Manhattan and the bright lights of Broadway at her doorstep, while she studied and taught acting.

While living at the Barbizon, she suffered two strokes. On October 26, 1932, the candle of her brilliant life quietly flickered and died. Margaret Brown was sixty-five years old.

Margaret's daughter, Helen, and her son, Lawrence, arranged a funeral with a Catholic Mass in Hempstead, Long Island, where Helen lived. Margaret was buried next to J. J. in Westbury, Long Island. Neither of the Browns were buried in their chosen home of Colorado, where they had found fortune in a mine called the Little Jonny and found love and happiness in their lives and their hearts.

In December of the year Margaret died, a special parcel arrived in Leadville. She had never forgotten her Leadville roots and often sent gifts and needed supplies to the mining families there during the holidays. This year was no different. Before she died, she made arrangements for her annual shipment of presents to arrive in Leadville before Christmas. Her nephew, Ted Brown, distributed candy, clothing, and seven hundred pairs of socks to needy miners and their families—a final gift from Mrs. J. J. Brown.

8 Molly Brown Myths

How did the Unsinkable Mrs. J. J. Brown become known as "Molly Brown" to so many people? Margaret Brown, her character and her story, were bigger than life. Some newspaper writers in the 1930s tried to change her story. It must have been a challenge to make it better than it had been in real life.

On October 28, 1932, two days after Margaret died, a retrospective article about her life appeared in the *Rocky Mountain News.* Margaret was called Molly several times in the article. With a colorful flair of the pen, young Margaret was described as a tomboy cavorting on the banks of the Missouri River who dove headfirst into a mud bank and was saved by Mark Twain. Her age at death was stated as 59 instead of 65. She supposedly showed up in Leadville at fifteen years of age and took work as a "pot rustler," or camp cook. More details told of J. J.'s offer to set up drinks for all who would "belly up to the bar."

Another story related how newlywed, newly rich J. J. Brown rushed home clutching $300,000 to present to his wife. Unknown to him, Maggie placed the bills inside their wood-burning stove for safekeeping. Later, when J. J. lit the stove, and the dollars went up in flames, he was unruffled. He said he could get plenty more where that came from. The truth is that coins, not paper dollars, were the most commonly used currency of the time. Little money was lost in the mishap.

Many of these tales, and others, found their way to the 1960 Broadway musical and later the movie about her life, *The Unsinkable Molly Brown.* Newspapers' use of the name "Molly" indicates that it was created much earlier, as early as 1932. One popular myth was that the name, Maggie, was changed to Molly to provide a more melodic word for the musical. Another myth said that Margaret wished people would call her Molly, but it never caught on. However, if Margaret wanted to be called by another name, no doubt she would have insisted on it herself.

So many people viewed and enjoyed the popular musical, that Margaret Brown became known as Molly

Brown to the American public. As sometimes happens with legends, the name has been repeated so often that it is accepted as her real name. It has become difficult to separate truth from myth regarding Mrs. J. J. Brown's life. Research and common sense are our best tools for separating the two.

THE FINEST STEAMER IN THE WORLD

48,328 TONS
DECLARED "UNSINKABLE"

One First Class Ticket to New York City, USA Parlor Suite - £870

DEPARTING FROM SOUTHAMPTON
APRIL 10, 1912
With Stops in Cherbourg, France and Queenstown, Ireland

Margaret Brown was fond of saying that a person she admired had a heart "as big as a ham." Whether it was a legend or not, it sounds like a phrase she would use. It is safe to say that Margaret Brown had a heart as big as a ham.

Timeline

1854 – James Joseph "J. J." Brown is born in Wymart, Pennsylvania.

1865 – The American Civil War ends.

1867 – Margaret Tobin is born on July 18 in Hannibal, Missouri.

1876 – Colorado achieves statehood.

1880 – James Joseph (J. J.) Brown arrives in Leadville.

1883 – Margaret's sister, Mary, and her husband, Jack Landrigan, move to Leadville, Colorado.

1886 – Margaret Tobin arrives in Leadville. Margaret marries J. J. Brown on September 1 in the Church of the Annunciation.

1887 – The Browns' first child, Lawrence (Larry), is born.

1889 – A second child, Catherine Ellen (Helen), is born.

1893 – An economic crisis hits the United States due to a slump in the price of silver. Woman's suffrage becomes law. Colorado is the second state after Wyoming to allow women to vote.

1894 – The Browns purchase their 1340 Pennsylvania Avenue home in Denver.

1896 – Margaret becomes a charter member of the Denver Woman's Club.

1898 – J. J. Brown suffers a mild stroke and semi-retires from mining.

1901 – Margaret Brown attends the Carnegie Institute.

1902 – The Browns travel around the world.

1909 – Margaret and J. J. Brown file for a formal separation. Their marriage is over.

1912 – The *Titanic* ocean liner sinks during its maiden voyage. Margaret Brown survives the tragedy.

1913 – Margaret campaigns for a nomination to run for Congress.

1914 – Ludlow Massacre takes place in southern Colorado. Margaret withdraws her Congressional campaign efforts.

1917 – The United States enters World War I.

1918 – World War I ends.

1922 – J. J. Brown dies on September 5.

1924 – Margaret Brown helps establish the first all-female "feminist coalition" for mine operations in Leadville.

1925 – Margaret Brown leads people to safety during a fire at the Breakers Hotel in Palm Beach, Florida.

1929 – Margaret Brown is awarded the Palm of the Academy of France for her theatrical work in *L'Aiglon.* Stock market crashes, which leads to the Great Depression.

1932 – Margaret Brown receives the French Legion of Honor award for her work during World War I and for being an "overall good citizen." Margaret dies on October 26 in New York City.

1960 – *The Unsinkable Molly Brown* musical begins performances on Broadway.

1962 – The movie, *The Unsinkable Molly Brown,* starring Debbie Reynolds, is released. Hollywood's Mrs. Brown is known forever after as "Unsinkable Molly Brown."

1970 – Molly Brown House in Denver is restored into a museum through the efforts of Historic Denver, Inc. and Colorado's first lady Ann Daniels Love.

Glossary

activist – a person who donates time and energy to causes they believe in, especially political causes

boomtown – a town that experiences a brief explosion in population due to mining or other industry

Congress – the legislative branch of United States government consisting of the Senate and House of Representatives

court – an old-fashioned word for dating

cyclone – a rotating windstorm of immense force

dry goods – clothing, fabric, and household merchandise for sale in a store

euchre – a card game for two, three, or four players, using the thirty-two highest cards in a deck

formidable – causing fear and dread

Irish Potato Famine – the peried from 1845 to 1849 when the potato crop in Ireland was killed by a fungus. Because the Irish people depended on the potato for food, at least 500,000 people died of starvation. The famine caused a great migration of the Irish to other countries.

kimonos – garments or loose robes worn by men and women in Japan

legends – great stories that cannot be proven, but are repeated so often that people begin to think they are true and the stories become a tradition

militia – a group of people trained in combat and military procedures available to defend the state against enemy aggression or in other emergencies

pen name – a name adopted by an author used to identify his or her published work

philanthropist – a person who donates money to worthy causes

principle – an idea upon which rules of behavior and conduct are built

progressive – making changes or improvements

siblings – brothers and sisters

strike – a work stoppage to call attention to a dispute between workers and managers

ukulele – a small four-stringed Hawaiian instrument played like a small guitar

widow – a woman whose husband has died

widower – a man whose wife has died

wireless radio – a radio that allowed telegraphic communication without wires as invented by Guglielmo Marconi

woman's suffrage – the right of women to vote in elections

yodeling – Swiss folk singing with sudden changes from low to high tones

Bibliography

Abbott/Leonard/McComb. *Colorado: A History of the Centennial State,* Niwot, Colorado: University Press of Colorado, 1982, pp. 370–371.

Ayer, Eleanor, H. *Colorado Chronicles v. 2–Famous Colorado Women,* Frederick: Jende-Hagan Bookcorp, 1982, pp. 22–25.

Bancroft, Caroline. *The Unsinkable Mrs. Brown,* Boulder, Johnson Books, 1961.

Blair, Edward and Churchill, E. Richard, *Everybody Came to Leadville,* First Light Publishing, Fort Collins, Colorado, 1997, pp. 30–33.

Brown, Lawrence P. [manuscript] Letters, photos, and business papers, Colorado Historical Society, MSS #84, box 4.

Brown, Margaret Tobin. 1928-1932 [manuscript] Letters to housekeeper, Mrs. Ella Grable, Denver Public Library, Western History Department, C MSS WH53 Rg1; Sec1; Sf4; Bx1.

Colorado Prospector, April and May, 1971.

Denver Post, April 15, 16, 17, 19, 27, 1912.

Denver Post, May 19, 1912.

Denver Post, October 28, 1932, pp. 1, 3.

Denver Post, October 29, 1932, p. 2.

Denver Times (Rocky Mountain News), April 15, 16, 19, 20, 1912.

Denver Times (Rocky Mountain News), May 1, 2, 19, 1912.

Denver Times (Rocky Mountain News), August 19, 1912.

Denver Woman's Press Club, "Who's Who In the Denver Woman's Press Club" 1898-1987 [manuscript], Denver Public Library, Western History Department, C MSS WH957 Rg7A;Sec7;Sf6;OVBx1.

Goldstein, Marcia Tremmel. *Denver Women in Their Places,* Denver: Historic Denver, Inc., 2002, pp. 42–44.

Iverson, Kristen. *Molly Brown, Unraveling the Myth,* Boulder: Johnson Books, 1999.

Leonard, Stephen J. and Thomas J. Noel. *Denver, Mining Camp to Metropolis,* Niwot: University Press of Colorado, 1990.

McAlester, Virginia and Lee, *A Field Guide to America's Historic Neighborhoods and Museum Houses—The Western States,* Alfred A Knopf, New York, 1998, pp. 300–302.

New York Times, Obituary for Margaret T. Brown, October 28, 1932, p. 19.

Noel, Thomas J., and Barbara S. Norren. *Denver, The City Beautiful,* Denver: Historic Denver, Inc., 1987.

Noel, Thomas J. *The Colorado Almanac,* Portland: West Winds Press, 2001, pp. 34–35.

Rocky Mountain News, March 4, 1927, p. 1.

Rocky Mountain News, October 28, 1932, pp. 1, 20.

Rocky Mountain News, April 6, 1941, p. 10.

Rocky Mountain News, December 8, 1949, pp. 5, 9.

Sampson, Joanna. *Remember Ludlow!* Denver: Colorado Historical Society, 1999.

Sherrow, Victoria. *Titanic,* New York: Scholastic Reference, 2001.

1870 U.S. Census, First Ward, Hannibal, Marion Co., Missouri, p. 18, line 24, John Tobin.

Web Sites

Colorado's Main Streets, http://www.cdpheritage.org/mainstreets/mollybrown.htm

Denver Public Library, *"Ask the Librarian",* http://www.denver.lib.co.us/

Dr. Colorado, Prof. Tom Noel, http://www.coloradowebsites.com/dr-colorado/

Encyclopedia Titanica, http://www.encyclopedia-titanica.org/firstclass/

Molly Brown House Museum, Historic Denver, http://www.mollybrown.org

Molly Brown Birthplace & Museum, Hannibal, Missouri, http://www.mollybrownmuseum.com

Molly Brown Summer House Museum, Lakewood, Colorado http://www.mollybrownsummerhousehistory.org/print molly and jj brown.htm

Park People: The Eugene Field House, http://www.theparkpeople.com/eugene.htm

Sanctuaries in the City: History and Mystery Abound At Denver's Catholic Church, by Colleen Smith, http://www.frontrangeliving.com/escapes/Cathedral.htm

Women of the West Museum, Margaret "Molly" Tobin Brown (1867-1932), http://www.autry-museum.org/explore/exhibits/lodo/molly.htm

Other Resources

Historic Denver's "Molly's Mystery Tour" on August 27, 2005, a tour of Leadville and the sites of Molly Brown's early years in Colorado. A booklet for the tour contains historical information summarized by biographer Kristin Iverson, including a copy of the Browns' marriage certificate.

Molly Brown House Museum, tour with Kerri Atter, Director, on March 23, 2006. Museum located at 1340 Pennsylvania Street, Denver, CO 80203, 303-832-4092. Hours: June 1–August 31, Monday to Saturday, 10 a.m.–4 pm.; Sunday, 12–4 p.m. September 1–May 31: Hours remain the same except closed on Monday. Closed on major holidays.

Index

Acknowledgments

I could not carry on and preserve the stories of our pioneers without the help and support of my family, friends, and publisher, and especially, without the unwavering support of my husband, Don. I am also fortunate to have valuable research facilities available in Denver. James Jeffrey and the crew in the Western History Collection at Denver Public Library are treasures. Librarians across the street at the Stephen A. Hart Library at the Colorado Historical Society are gems. Kerri Atter, Director, Molly Brown House Museum, shared her time and expertise to provide valuable direction and encouragement. Mary Rose Garland Shearer continues her family's tradition of preserving the Molly Brown Summer House. Author and researcher Patricia Werner guided me to the right place at the right time. Vicki Dempsey reached out from the Molly Brown Birthplace & Museum in Hannibal with her help, expertise, and a great photo. I thank all who helped me locate the spirit of the real Margaret Tobin Brown.

About the Author

Award-winning author, Joyce B. Lohse, grew up in Illinois where she sometimes spent her school recess time writing stories and poems. She is the author of a dual biography of Colorado's first governor and his wife entitled, *First Governor, First Lady: John and Eliza Routt of Colorado*. She is happiest when researching and writing about pioneers of the West for her books in the "Now You Know Bio" series. Learn more about Joyce Lohse and her work at www.lohseworks.com

More
Now You Know Bios

Justina Ford:
Medical Pioneer
ISBN: 0-86541-074-7
$8.95
Joyce B. Lohse

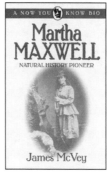

Martha Maxwell:
Natural History Pioneer
ISBN: 978-0-86541-075-6
$8.95
James McVey

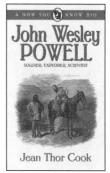

John Wesley Powell:
Soldier Explorer Scientist
ISBN: 978-0-86541-080-0
$8.95
Jean Thor Cook

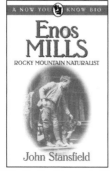

Enos Mills: Rocky Mountain Naturalist
ISBN: 978-0-86541-072-5 $8.95
John Stansfield

Emily Griffith: Opportunity's Teacher
ISBN: 978-0-86541-077-0 $8.95
Joyce B. Lohse

Now You Know Bios are available at your local bookstore,
by calling 888.570.2663, and online at
www.filterpressbooks.com